# Praying the Rosary

## The Joyful, Fruitful, Sorrowful, and Glorious Mysteries

*Warren Dicharry, C.M.*

*A Liturgical Press Book*

THE LITURGICAL PRESS
Collegeville, Minnesota

Cover design by Kathryn Brewer.

| 1 | 2 | 3 | 4 | 5 | 6 | 7 | 8 |
|---|---|---|---|---|---|---|---|

Library of Congress Cataloging-in-Publication Data

Dicharry, Warren F.
    Praying the rosary : the joyful, fruitful, sorrowful, and glorious mysteries / Warren Dicharry.
        p.    cm.
    ISBN 0-8146-2484-7 (alk. paper)
    1. Rosary.   2. Mysteries of the rosary.    3. Catholic Church—Prayer-books and devotions—English.    I. Title.
BX2163.D54    1998
242'.74—dc21                                            97-34281
                                                               CIP

*To all the many who pray the Rosary.*
*Who strive to meditate its Mysteries.*
*This **"labor of love"** is dedicated.*

# Contents

# Preface

When our brief candle is wasted and this body is laid to final rest, someone may very carefully wrap a rosary around our hands. It is our proper rest. Only thus can we slip decently into the next life. Only thus are we ready to meet our Maker. Whether or not we ever prayed the Rosary during our life, whether the Rosary ever nestled gently in our hands, often our relatives and friends would not consider it fitting to bury us in any other way.

Thus, a rosary is our adornment in burial. But additionally, it seems to me, the Rosary is being said more now than ever before. Perhaps, it is the result of pilgrimages to Lourdes, Fatima, or Medjugorje. Perhaps, it is the near approach of the third millennium, with its wars, earthquakes, tornadoes, and hurricanes. What can we expect tomorrow? We do not know, but at least we can say the Rosary, and we shall feel safe.

Whether the Rosary was propagated by St. Dominic during the Albigensian heresy, for which there seems to be no tangible proof, or whether the Church took an age-old practice, the beads, and fitted them to one hundred and fifty to correspond to the number of psalms being recited daily or weekly by the clergy is unclear. This was a time of faith, while the ordinary laity were largely illiterate, so that the Rosary served their needs quite nicely.

Why then another book on the Rosary? What purpose does it tend to serve? Just two, but two that justify the writing of a whole book. First, I cannot help feeling that most Catholics who pray the Rosary pay attention to the Hail Mary's rather than to the mysteries. The Rosary is primarily a Christian rather than a Marian devotion. We Catholics are to pray it by meditation on the mysteries during the time it takes to say ten Hail Marys. Sadly, we clergy never seem to get around to teaching just how to meditate on the Joyful, Sorrowful, and Glorious Mysteries. My first purpose in writing this book, then, is to offer means of meditating on the mysteries by providing three things for each of the mysteries: (1) a description of the site, which I have visited and examined, usually more than once; (2) an interpretation of the Scripture texts, since I have taught Scripture, both the Old and New Testament, for some thirty years; and (3) a practical reflection on the subject of each mystery for personal benefit. Obviously, I cannot include everything that the mystery will suggest, but I can certainly include enough to make meditation on the particular mystery worthwhile. In fact, on individual days, the site, the Scripture text, and the reflection can each be the matter of meditation. In other words, it is not necessary to exhaust the whole content on each occasion.

The second purpose of this book is more complicated. When you stop to think about it, do you realize that we pass directly from the Infancy Gospels of Matthew and Luke to the Passion, thoroughly skipping three full years of public ministry? Perhaps, once it was necessary to do that in order to correspond to the one hundred and fifty psalms, but our situation is now changed. Most of us are literate and can read the psalms if we wish. So why not include the years of Jesus' public life? I call these Fruitful or Spirited Mysteries, but a better term may be borrowed if it can be thought of. What I have done with the Fruitful or Spirited Mysteries is easily seen in the choices and changes I have made. Take the *kerygma* (the public proclamation of the Church which underlies all four Gospels and the principal discourses in Acts) and change them somewhat, thus (1) the Baptism and Witness of Jesus, (2) the Galilean Ministry, notably the Sermon on the Mount, (3) the Transfiguration, (4) the Journey to Jerusalem, to which Luke devotes ten whole chapters, and (5) the Last Night of Jesus' life, when he instituted the Eucharist and the New Covenant and gave his last discourse. That then leads directly into the Prayer and Agony of Jesus, with which the Sorrowful Mysteries begin.

But what about distributing the mysteries on the different days of the week, with the first mysteries on Monday and Thursday, with the second mysteries on Tuesday and Friday, and the third mysteries on Wednesday, Saturday, and Sunday? What I suggest is to omit the Sunday mystery, substituting the Joyful Mysteries, then the Fruitful on Monday, the Sorrowful on Tuesday, and the Glorious on Wednesday. Thus, if Mysteries are said each day, there will be adequate time once a week for the Fruitful or Spirited Mysteries.

Before beginning the Rosary proper, we are expected to say one Apostles Creed, one Our Father, and three Hail Marys in honor of the Trinity or Mary's three virtues of humility, purity, and love. Since Catholics generally know these basic prayers, let us assume that these are already well known, as are also the Our Father at the beginning of each decade, the Gloria at the end of each decade, the "Dear Jesus, forgive us of our sins, save us from the fires of hell, lead all souls to heaven, especially those in most need of your mercy," and the Hail Holy Queen at the end. That leaves us nothing to handle, then, except the Joyful, Fruitful, Sorrowful, and Glorious Mysteries, to which this work is principally dedicated.

In so far as is possible, I shall endeavor to devote one page each to the description of the site involved, one page to the interpretation of the Scriptures concerned, and one page to the detailing of the practical and spiritual reflections suggested by the particular mystery. And may my readership derive as much spiritual profit from the reading of this little book as I have derived from writing it.

Before concluding this preface, I want to express my deepest gratitude to Mrs. Sarah Pantoja for voluntarily typing the manuscript at a time when my own initiative was severely curtailed by cataract operations.

Warren F. Dicharry, C.M.
Vincentian Evangelization
Holy Trinity Catholic Church
Dallas, Texas

# I.

# The Joyful Mysteries

## 1. The Annunciation of the Angel to Mary

Of all the shrines devoted to our Lady, there is none so beautiful than that of the Annunciation, found at Nazareth, in Galilee. First, however, it is necessary to describe Nazareth, which is laid out like an outdoor theater, stone houses replacing benches, and stone alley ways or "aisles" running up the hills so steep that some even have steps in them. In the center of that reminder of an outdoor theater stands the new gleaming white Basilica of the Annunciation or Incarnation. Entering through a side door to the interior, we are filled with admiration over the main or parochial part, sitting beneath the fluted dome, with the huge painting of Mary and the Church covering the wall behind the main altar. Through the *oculus* or eye in the floor directly under the fluted dome, we become aware of the lower floor, even more important than the upper one, which we promptly examine by means of one of the three stairways. First, an abundance of beautiful national shrines greets us, then the ancient grotto, the most sacred object of veneration in the entire shrine. Everything about the grotto inspires awe, but especially the inscription on the front of the altar containing the unforgettable words, "Verbum caro hic factum est" ("The Word was made flesh HERE").

We will be seeing and venerating the star of the nativity in Bethlehem, and worthy of highest praise it is, but can anything surpass the very spot where the incarnation took place, where, with the consent of Mary, the Word became flesh in her womb? Let us pause here to praise the Son of God and to venerate his Holy Mother.

The pertinent Scripture text is the account of the Annunciation in Luke 1:26-38, in which Luke has the angel Gabriel divulge a triple revelation, to each of which Mary responds. Because there is so much material in this section, I will explain the angel's revelation first and then use Mary's responses to direct our conduct.

"Hail, favored one! The Lord is with you." This manner of greeting recalls two messianic prophecies, Zephaniah 3:14 and Zechariah 2:14, both of which congratulate Sion (Jerusalem), for God is within her.

> Do not be afraid, Mary, for you have found favor with God. Behold, you will conceive in your womb and bear a son, and you shall name him Jesus. He will be great and will be called Son of the Most High, and the Lord God will give him the throne of David his father, and he will rule over the house of Jacob forever, and of his kingdom there will be no end.

In this section Gabriel alludes to the messianic prophesies of Isaiah 7:14 and 2 Samuel 7:14, while referring also to the coronation psalms (in the nineties).

> The holy Spirit will come upon you, and the power of the Most High will overshadow you. Therefore, the child to be born will be called holy, the Son of God. And behold, Elizabeth, your relative, has also conceived a son in her old age, and this is the sixth month for her who is called barren; for nothing is impossible for God.

This section contains, as if in outline form, the climax of the entire announcement. "The Holy Spirit" connotes the creative act of Genesis 1:2, while the "power of the Most

High" recalls to mind the wanderings of his Holy People in the desert, for *episkiádso* ("overshadow") is the Septuagint translation of Hebrew *shakan*, of which the noun form is *Shekinah* (Exod 40:34-39). Also *to hágion* is both neuter for "the child" and stands for "the holy place," the temple referred to in John 1:14, 2:21.

As I explained earlier, I have divided the Annunciation into two—the angel's announcement in one and Mary's profound responses in the other. Mary's *responses,* which are very appropriate to us, are also three-fold, as follows.

"But she was greatly troubled at what was said and pondered what sort of greeting this might be." Mary's *humility* immediately comes into view. She simply cannot understand how and why she should be greeted in such a unique way.

"How can this be, since I have no relation with a man?" After her humility, *purity* becomes the most outstanding virtue. And, all through her life, her inviolate purity rests on solid ground, for she is "our tainted nature's solitary boast" (Wadsworth, "The Virgin").

"Behold, I am the handmaid of the Lord. May it be done to me according to your word." This third and final response of Mary indicates total, self-surrendering gift of self through unconditional *love.* A word should be said here about love. In our English language, we have only the one word for love, which has to make do in every conceivable situation, but in Greek, the language of the New Testament, there are three distinct words: *éros,* "passionate love," such as that of marriage; *philía,* "friendship," connoting a certain equality between the friends; and *agápe,* divine love, shared with men and women. It is mainly this final type that is spoken of in the New Testament, and we must always advert to its supreme, unlimited, divine, unconditional characteristics if we wish to be transformed into Christ.

For Americans, let me point out that the flower of humility is *blue,* the violet; the flower of purity is *white,* the Easter lily; and the flower of love is *red,* the red, red rose. Put together, they are the red, white, and blue of our flag, dedicated to Mary, as indicated by the national shrine in Washington. To be American means to be Christian, for excellence.

## 2. The Visitation of Mary to Elizabeth

Tradition has identified the beautiful event of the Visitation with an equally beautiful location just west of Jerusalem, known as Ain Karim, the "Vineyard Spring." This lovely site really consists of two distinct parts, two principal churches marking the two edges of a picturesque valley. One, that of the Spanish-style Church of St. John the Baptist, is characterized by the ancient grotto of John's birth and Zechariah's hymn of praise. The other is that of the Italian-style Church of the Visitation where Elizabeth was staying during her pregnancy when visited by Mary.

In contrast with the Church of St. John, that of the Visitation is noteworthy for its solitude, silence, and aptness for prayer. First, on the facade of the building is the most beautiful mosaic portrayal of Mary on her donkey, accompanied by angels, riding from Nazareth in Galilee to Ain Karim in Judea. Such a journey may not seem so difficult to us today, but whether alone or in a caravan, such a trip would have been a major undertaking at the time. Next, as one enters the building, one is immediately transfixed by the striking picture of Mary reciting her Magnificat, which speaks of her humility, her lowliness before God, who alone is worthy of all praise and who unfailingly lifts up the poor while he brings to nothing the wealthy. On the wall opposite the windows rests a whole collection of magnificent frescoes depicting incidents in the life of Mary and Jesus. Finally, in the lower church, on the wall opposite the windows, there exist in beautiful metal frames the Magnificat in many of the world's languages, with spaces for more still. Thus, we have the perfect location for honoring Jesus through Mary.

The Scripture texts offer two levels of thought for our meditation: (1) that which consists in the things said by Elizabeth and by Mary, i.e., the famous Magnificat, and (2) that which is drawn from the spiritual meaning of the incident. Let's take them in that order.

Mary, carrying the child Jesus in her womb, and thinking only of Elizabeth's needs, hastens to the hill country of Judah to help in whatever way possible. She greets Elizabeth and rejoices to hear her cousin's extraordinary words, "Most blessed are you among women, and blessed is the fruit of your womb. . . . Blessed are you who *believed* that what was spoken to you by the Lord would be fulfilled" (Luke 1:43, 45, emphasis added), providing part of the text of the *Hail Mary* (Judg 13:18). Mary responds with her glorious hymn of praise, known as the Magnificat.

The secret of the spiritual interpretation of this section of Scripture lies in 2 Samuel 6. David, now ruling all Israel, has also conquered Jerusalem and desires to make it his religious as well as his political capital, but for that purpose he needs to bring the ark of the covenant into the city. Where is the ark? Ever since its capture by the Philistines and its return by them to Israel (I Sam 4–6), the ark has rested in Kiriath-Yearim at the home of the priest, Abinadab. So while David and his followers are bringing the ark to Jerusalem with great jubilation, Uzzah, one of Abinadab's sons, reaches out to steady the ark and is struck dead. Whereupon David exclaims, "Who am I that the ark of the LORD should come to me?" (2 Sam 6:9) and has it diverted to the house of Obededom. After three months, during which God blesses Obededom, David finally receives the ark, leaping and dancing for joy in its presence. Study carefully the points of contact in these episodes.

For our reflection, the Visitation account proposes, first, *charity to our neighbor.* No sooner had the angel left her than Mary's first thought was of visiting her cousin Elizabeth, six months pregnant, in the hill country of Judah. This she did without the least thought of danger or fatigue. And so must be our own dispositions.

But the response of Elizabeth is extraordinary: Mary is blessed among women and blessed is her child, and who is she to receive the (Ark) Mother of her Lord? This identification of the Mother of God and the ark of the covenant is worthy of much reflection. And in confirmation, it is noteworthy that, in Revelation 12, that great central figure of the end times, the sign of the coming of the "woman clothed with the sun" is none other than the ark of the covenant (Rev 11:19).

Third, the virtue *Faith* is certainly inculcated here, but not primarily clinging to belief in something against all odds, but rather in a biblical sense faith as a total, unconditional gift of self. We are to believe in God *(in deum)* with our total self and with no intention of "indian giving."

Our best chance of meditating on Zechariah's Benedictus and on Mary's Magnificat lies in reading them slowly and meditating on their powerful content. However, we can at least give a clue. Read I Samuel 2: 1-10, for it seems to provide the background for the Magnificat and to some extent also for the Benedictus. Second, concentrate on *humility* as being the most crucial virtue. As St. Vincent de Paul used to love to express it so well and so often, "If we haven't got humility, we haven't got anything!" All else pales before God unless we have the knowledge, the truth, the wisdom that he and he alone is the author of everything positive in our spiritual life. Sin alone comes directly from us, and a lifetime is needed to atone for sin.

## 3. The Nativity of the Lord

Bethlehem, meaning "House of Bread," sits serenely on a low mountain peak, some six miles south of Jerusalem and four miles northwest of the Herodium. The Herodium, the lofty "burial mound" of Herod the Great seeking earthly glory, once stood proud and haughty among the public and religious buildings of Israel. Now, the Herodium is an abandoned *khirbet* ("ruin"), while Bethlehem continues to grow and shine as one of the most picturesque of the Holy Land.

After viewing Bethlehem from the Shepherds' Field, we go into Manger Square and enter the fourth-century basilica (the oldest active church in Christendom?) through its tiny door. An earlier full-size door was an open invitation to enemies of the Church to ride in on their horses and make fun of the church.

The first church from the fourth century that we encounter is the Greek Orthodox with the various patches of the original frescoes giving the secret of preserving unity. And then we pass by the original grotto that honors the birth of the Savior. What a feeling comes over one! Here we are standing by the very star, a silver star, marking the spot of Jesus' birth and the altar of the manger. Though the manger itself is shown in the Basilica of St. Mary Major in Rome, here we are at the very spot of the birth and the laying in the manger of the Savior, and we can only say, "How great thou art."

Here we need to stand or kneel very still and reconstruct the birth of Jesus in our minds and hearts. For this we have the infancy Gospels of Matthew and Luke to draw from. They complement each other, although all we can rely on as historically true is what they have in common, that Jesus was born of a virgin in Bethlehem.

Fortunately for us, the Nativity of Jesus is accompanied by extensive Scripture readings. Even if we omit St. Luke's expression about the birth of Jesus, we still have the Gospel of Matthew, which provides the human genealogy, first of Joseph the Dreamer, then the Holy Family at home in Bethlehem, the visit of the Magi from the East, the slaughter of the Innocents, the flight into Egypt, the call from Egypt, and the growing up in fabled Nazareth. Did all this happen as Matthew puts it? Perhaps not. Remember this is all part of the work of Gospel interpretation, dating from the desire for the glory of God and the encouragement of man, not dealing according to the word and example of Jesus, but with an infancy narrative designed to show the connections including Jesus' sojourn with his own people.

By the same token, it becomes evident that the second Lukan narrative is of Jesus born for all people, including shepherds and other poor people. Thus Matthew, who wants to show Jesus as endowment of Israel, depicts him as a son of David, indeed of Israel, as working all kinds of miracles, even from his birth, and of fulfilling all the messianic prophecies of Israel. Luke, by contrast, who will later recount all those famous dramatic parables, here begins by showing him to be the universal Savior, especially of the poor and less fortunate among both men and women. In both infancy Gospels Jesus is described in such a way that we can easily see what he will be and even now, by Matthew's quotes and Luke's allusions, Jesus will be the extraordinary Son of God and Savior of the world, especially for those in most need of his help (e.g., the shepherds). In being born at Bethlehem, Jesus showed his predilection for humility, poverty, and love for the lowliest people.

For the application of Scripture to our personal spiritual life, no more than a little meditation is needed, especially if we meditate on the Scriptures. In Matthew's Gospel, let us undertake to be one of the Wise Men from the East who have been given a portion of the truth, but now seek it entirely. Taking upon ourselves the greatest of difficulties and wandering steadily onward, we press on until our faith is rewarded by the discovery of him who is Son of God and King of Israel. In Luke's Gospel, we unite ourselves with the simple and humble shepherds and go to Bethlehem to find the Holy Child and worship him. Richard Crashaw, the great English poet, so honored the Christ-Child with these words:

> Welcome, all wonders in one sight.
> Eternity shut in a span:
> Summer in winter, day in night,
> Heaven in earth and God in man.
> Great little One,
> Whose all-embracing birth
> Lifts earth to Heaven,
> Stoops Heaven to earth.

The virtues principally manifested by Jesus at his birth are humility, poverty, and love. Remember the little door of our entrance? That is our symbol, that Jesus, the Son of God, and God himself became a tiny, helpless baby! What humility, what love! And lay in a manger. What poverty! "For your sake he became poor although he was rich, so that by his poverty you might become rich" (2 Cor 8:9). He traded the glories of God for the abject poverty and humility of a son of man and servant of YHWH.

## 4. The Presentation of Jesus in the Temple

It is beautiful and impressive now. It must have been extremely so in the first century of our era. Now, for example, there lies an entire square of walkways, a few trees, various places for washing hands and feet, a lively mosque for worship, once named St. John the Evangelist but now called *el-Aksa* ("the distant one"), and finally the Dome of the Rock, where theoretically Jews, Christians, and Muslims can side by side venerate the rock on which our common ancestor Abraham attempted to sacrifice his dear son Isaac (Gen 22). I say "theoretically" because there is still so much strong feeling among members of the three great religions, and they are far from agreement. What was meant to bring them together has succeeded in alienating them perhaps forever.

Nothing remains today of the magnificent Temple of Herod the Great, which should be considered as one of the seven wonders of the world. It dominated Jerusalem, Israel, and the thought processes of much of the contemporary world. In the time of Jesus, the Temple was well constructed, though not yet finished, by Herod. What later was to be largely open was entirely covered. Each section (holy of holies, holy place, court of the faithful, court of the women, and court of the Gentiles) was complete in its own way and carefully distinguished from the other courts. Underneath it all were the stables of Solomon, where those involved with the Temple could keep their horses and other animals while they were busy going about their duties. Mary and Joseph, of course, came to the Temple out of duty but received prophecies as well, prophecies that would not only concern them but all of Israel.

There is much in this mystery to think about. I have mentioned that here we meditate on our consecration, and this, in both Testaments, is one of the most meaningful words in all of Scripture. There are two places in particular in the Old Testament, that speak to us about the importance of consecration.

The first is the story of Samson in the book of Judges 13–16. He was consecrated from his mother's womb, and as long as he was faithful to his consecration, he was a superman, doing all kinds of prodigies. But once he gave away to Delilah, the Philistine prostitute, the secret of his consecration, he became as weak as any of us. He was captured by the Philistines, his eyes were torn out, and he was put to treading out grain like any animal. But the Philistines neglected to keep cutting his hair. It grew back and with it grew Samson's reconsecration, whereby he was able to pull down the whole temple of Dagon, the god of the Philistines, on their royalty and people, killing more Philistines in his death than in his life.

The second place is in Daniel 5, the story of Belshazzar, throwing a banquet, or rather an orgy for himself, his courtiers, and their women. Precisely at the point when he determines to bring in the sacred vessels brought by Nebuchadnezzar from the Temple in Jerusalem, he sees the handwriting on the wall, "Mene, mene, thekal, upharsim." Suspecting a bad omen, he calls in his wise men, who read it as nouns; the names of coins. Only when he calls in Daniel does he get a true meaning as verbs, *Mene:* "God has numbered your kingdom and put an end to it." *Theke:* "You have been weighed on the scales and found wanting." *Peres:* "Your kingdom has been divided and given to the Medes and Persians." And that very night, the city fell to the Medes and Persians.

It must be remembered that, on this Feast of the Presentation, Mary and Joseph, being faithful Jews, were fulfilling the words of Scripture, recorded in Exodus 13:1-2, 15:

The LORD spoke to Moses and said, "Consecrate to me every first-born that opens the womb among the Israelites, both of man and beast, for it belongs to me." When Pharaoh stubbornly refused to let us go, the LORD killed every first-born in the land of Egypt, every first-born of man and of beast. That is why I sacrifice to the LORD everything of the male sex that opens the womb and why I redeem every first-born of my sons.

But, important as these words were in our understanding of the Feast of the Dedication, the words of Simeon were even more important. He was a good man, who had been promised that he would not die until he had seen the Messiah. Now, entering the Temple and gazing on Jesus, he broke out in these unforgettable words:

> Now, Master, you may let your servant go
>    in peace, according to your word,
> for my eyes have seen your salvation,
>    which you have prepared in sight of all the peoples,
> a light of revelation to the Gentiles,
>    and glory for your people Israel (Luke 2:29-32).

Then, after a brief interval, he declares further,

> Behold, this child is destined for the fall and rise of many in Israel, and to be a sign that will be contradicted (and you yourself [Mary] a sword will pierce) so that the thoughts of many hearts may be revealed (Luke 2:33-35).

And Anna, a holy widow, likewise spoke of Jesus to all Israel.

## 5. The Finding of Jesus in the Temple

Only once in Jesus' growing up years is he mentioned in the Bible. That is, of course, when he went to Jerusalem with Mary and Joseph, as was customary, when the child had reached his twelfth year, that is the year before his *bar mitzvah*. And so he is found after three days in the midst of the learned doctors of Israel, hearing them and asking them questions. Thus is shown who Jesus is, that he is more than human, and that he naturally finds his place to be among the learned ones of Israel, and it gives us, albeit briefly, a view of Jesus, the Son of God, acknowledging who his Father really is. And whether we understand the text as suggesting that he must be found in his Father's house or about his Father's business, the meaning remains the same, that Jesus is acknowledging his identity freely, that God himself is his Father.

Now, this can hardly be used as an argument for Jesus' knowledge of himself, since we are not in the *kerygma,* which does not begin until the chapter in each Gospel that speaks of his baptism by John the Baptist. What we have here, it is agreed by most Scripture scholars, is a *midrashic* (meditative) account of his life. This one incident alone in his growing up years is very important in showing his knowledge of who he is.

But, as we will see in a moment, even more importantly than this acknowledgment of who he is, is what follows it, namely the words about his Nazareth years, as indicating how he grew up, and what was important in view of the beginning of the *kerygma.*

Compared to the rest of the Joyous Mysteries of the Rosary, we do not find a great deal of Scripture to back up Jesus' declaration about himself, to the anxious query of Mary and Joseph for some explanation for his deliberately hiding from them, so that they had to go to the trouble of finding him after three whole days of questions and worry. They naturally did not understand his conduct. It was certainly unexpected, for they had raised him thus far in a purely natural fashion. Nothing in his background had prepared them for this. True, there had been the predictions of Simeon at his presentation in the Temple, but Mary and Joseph were the sole beneficiaries of these, and they were given no information about making these known to the child. So far as they knew and expected, the child was destined to grow up perfectly normal and, only when "his hour had come" would he make his true identity known.

This is indicated not only by their consternation but also by what follows. "He went down with them and came to Nazareth, and was obedient to them; and [Mary] kept all these things in her heart. And Jesus advanced [in] wisdom and age and favor before God and man" (Luke 2: 51-52).

These words are full of meaning. Jesus grew and developed at Nazareth for those thirty years in a perfectly normal fashion, except within. He was growing in his knowledge of Scripture and in his relationship with his Father, reaching the highest point of mystical union, so that at his baptism, he fully deserved to hear those unforgettable words, addressed directly to him in Mark's Gospel, "You are my beloved Son; with you I am well pleased" (1:11). This understanding of the text renders unnecessary the writing of apocryphal gospels, recounting all the miracles of Jesus during his growing years. There were none, for his growth was normal.

One would think that the lessons to be learned from the finding in the Temple should be applied only to children, but such is not the case. True it is that the lesson about obedience to our parents is applied especially to children. If the very Son of God was totally obedient to his parents, who are we to do otherwise? Of course, his earthly parents were none other than Mary and Joseph, but the lesson applies to all parents, except in cases in which they are obviously in the wrong. But the other lesson is far more universal.

We all have the opportunity and responsibility to grow up like Jesus, reaching the heights of the spiritual life like him, although we may do nothing extraordinary in our whole lifetime. All the growth, all the effort that we can give to our growing up is applied to the interior. God will not abandon us. God will certainly help us to grow as we should and need to, but he must see goodwill on our part. And how is this growth to take place? Well, if our union with God is what we mean by religion, then prayer, which is communication in this union with God, is the great means of growth. Not just prayer of petition, although *that too is most important for it acknowledges our complete dependence on God.* But personal, heart-to-heart prayer is what is most important here. I can remember learning about this kind of prayer when I was twelve years old, just like Jesus, but I had no guide, no one to keep me growing in the right direction, so I am afraid that my growth was stunted. And now, looking back from the age of seventy-seven, I see so many ways in which I could have grown to the fullness of the age of Christ. I thank God for finally tearing me away from worldly concerns and enabling me to grow before it is too late, but I deeply regret the time wasted.

# II.

# The Fruitful Mysteries

## 1. The Baptism of Jesus

Now we come to one of the most recognizable factors in all the Holy Bible—the River Jordan. Extending beyond Israel, it is part of the Great Rift, which shows up even in Ethiopia. Its initial form is easily recognizable by the profundity of its standing in the earth around it. Receiving its abundance of water from the Beka valley in Lebanon, the Sea of Galilee is six hundred feet below sea level at its height and thirteen hundred below sea level at its depth. The Jordan receives its abundance of water from the Sea of Galilee, but does not hoard it to itself. Rather it empties this water into the Dead Sea, which is thirteen hundred feet below sea level at its height and twenty-six hundred under sea level at its bottom. It is so deep that it no longer has an outlet. Its water evaporates, leaving more salt and other chemicals that are so extensive that in its southern part they look like icebergs floating around. The River Jordan just above the Dead Sea was the site of Jesus' baptism by John the Baptist. The Sea of Galilee, River Jordan, and Dead Sea form a beautiful parable. If like the Sea of Galilee and the Jordan, we do not hoard our spiritual gifts to ourselves, we always remain pure, rich, and alive. But if like the Dead Sea, we have no outlet, we always remain dead, life-less, and ugly.

The double chapel that the Franciscans built in 1935 to honor the Baptism of Jesus was so damaged by an earthquake on December 18, 1956, that it had to be dismantled and replaced by an outdoor enclosure.

The encomiums of Jesus at his baptism by John are mentioned in all the Gospels. Perhaps the most dramatic occurs in the first Gospel, that of St. Mark. In that Gospel the voice from heaven is addressed directly to Jesus. Not only that, but the Spirit, who appears in the form of a dove, flies into the very body of Jesus, and thus is with Jesus during his entire life. To appreciate this one has to read the entire Gospel with the realization that the Holy Spirit is within Jesus.

In all the Gospel narratives, however, the Holy Spirit is with Jesus, even though it is not as clear as in Mark's Gospel. In fact, not only the Holy Spirit but the presence of Jesus himself with us is very clear and obvious. This, of course, is one of the most important truths of the baptism of John as applied to us.

The importance of the Baptism of Jesus is evident from its occurrence in all four Gospels. In keeping with the transfiguration and the agony of Jesus, this forms a pattern in all the Gospels, especially the Synoptic Gospels. In fact, the more we consider the matter, the more evident it becomes to us that the Baptism of Jesus is central to our knowledge of Jesus in the Gospels. In fact, it is the first of the points in the *kerygma,* that is the public proclamation of the Church regarding Jesus in the Gospels.

Let us linger here, at the Baptism of Jesus, and contemplate all it meant to him and to us to be officially acknowledged by the Father himself.

So far as the application of the Baptism of Jesus to our personal spiritual life is concerned, let us always bear in mind that this is the first point of our *kerygma* and as such it becomes the first of our spiritual life, too. First, it is by baptism that we are introduced to the life of Jesus. Plainly, in our baptism, the pouring of the water over our head signified the washing away of all sin, that is true, but more than that it signifies the introduction of the life of Christ into our own life.

Moreover, there are anointings before and after the pouring of the water, each of which is very important. The first, which is optional, but always included by me because of its meaning, is to remind us of the practice of ancient antagonists in the Olympics and other popular games. It is an anointing with the oil of catechumens on the breast of child or adult, to remind us of the practice in the ancient days of anointing the whole *body* before athletic games. And it is precisely at that time that we remember our life-long struggle between living the life of the flesh or of the spirit throughout our life (Gal 5:16-26; Rom 8:1-13).

After the pouring of the water, we are anointed with the chrism, that sacred, perfumed ointment that makes us kings, priests, and prophets. But more importantly, it consecrates us to God, so that in later life, we can never be anything but dedicated to the divine. The story of Samson (Judges 13, 16) and the story of Belshazzar (Daniel 5) teach us our importance as consecrated to God. I am convinced that, if we fully realize our importance as consecrated people and fully live out our dignity, it will be much easier to become saints.

## 2. The Galilean Ministry of Jesus

The second aspect of this group of mysteries is concerned with the Galilean Ministry. However, in order to concentrate this general activity into a single whole, it would be well to pick out a particular place where the Galilean Ministry was especially practiced. And such a place exists, the site of the Sermon on the Mountain in Matthew and the Plain in Luke, the house of Peter, and the synagogue at Capernaum. Together it is called Capernaum, where Jesus fixed the headquarters of his Galilean Ministry, and a beautiful spot it certainly is.

The Church of the Beatitudes, constructed in 1938 by the famous Italian architect Barluzzi, is truly a thing of beauty. Arranged around a single dome, the main altar and the additional lesser altars, one for each of the beatitudes, are pleasantly placed so that the priest and people together might be able to enjoy this church.

Also at Capernaum near the Sea of Galilee, Peter's house, surrounded by an octagonal series of walls, rests serenely between the synagogue and the sea and serves to recall to the scholar or the pious person the many occasions in which Peter had spoken rashly.

Finally, standing in proud splendor, the synagogue is sufficient to recall to the reader, particularly Jesus' objections at the end of his long discourse on faith and the Eucharist at Capernaum. Of course, this is not the actual edifice in which Jesus discoursed on the Eucharist in John 6, but it had to be close by, for the Jews tended to construct new synagogues on the site of the old. Thus, behind the present synagogue are the ruins of a more ancient one, in the black stone of more ancient and cheaper structures in Israel.

What were Jesus' main purposes during his Galilean ministry? Was it not to show himself to be truly messianic in his thoughts, words, and acts? His was truly messianic ministry, especially in his great discourse, which we know as the Sermon on the Mount. Whether this is a real or a fictitious discourse, we know not, but it seems certain that he must have given longer discourses such as the Sermon on the Mount. It is, of course, on the Mount that Matthew shows Jesus' similarity to Moses, and on the plain that Luke shows Jesus as the Savior of all people.

The Beatitudes are unique, presenting Jesus' position concerning all affairs of the world. Then he instructs us to be the salt and light of the world. Today, these two figures have nothing in common, but in Jesus' day, they were indispensable. Then there is a series of things that show the superiority of Jesus' discipline to that of the Pharisees.

In Mark's Gospel, Jesus is first shown to be truly divine, and then to freely opt to suffer and die to save us from sin. Perhaps, it is best expressed in Mark 10:45, "The Son of Man did not come to be served but to serve and to give his life as a ransom for many."

In Matthew's Gospel (11:25-30) Jesus pleads with us to accept his yoke rather than that of the Pharisees. In Luke's Gospel, the broad dimension of Jesus' compassion is best shown.

In trying to find the most suitable applications of the above to our individual lives, I am overcome by the multiplicity of texts available. If some situations called for a miracle or a cure, then Jesus could take care of them right away and thus have time to continue on his way. But if the situation called for something of greater suffering or humiliation, then Jesus was also ready. It seems to me that, in answering our call to universal ministry, we find our best model in these chapters. There is never a one-sided approach to things. Rather, everything is met head-on with a well-balanced response. Jesus is the greatest example of the kind of ministry that he expects of us in our world.

In following Jesus' example in ministry, it is a joy to see in him all the perfection to be found in those early chapters of Matthew, in which we contemplate Jesus, counterbalancing everything he did with something else, so that there is never any judgment too high or wide for us to follow, but rather all things are held in balance.

But nowhere can we find our perfect example of ministry better than seeing Jesus in the Gospel of St. Luke. The most compassionate of men and yet at the same time the most demanding, Jesus gives himself as the perfect minister. Here we see him, honored a little less than the angels, but rising far above the angels in his universal love and forgiveness. And in John's Gospel, likewise, we see Jesus in the early chapters filled with foreboding of what is to come, but nevertheless, not at all stepping back from what his Father was asking of him. What a perfect example to us!

## 3. The Transfiguration of the Lord

Now we come to one of the most dramatic episodes of Jesus' ministry, one which was marked by graphic accounts in the Synoptic Gospels and referred to analogously in John's Gospel, the story of the Transfiguration of Jesus "on a very high mountain." As to the identification of the mountain, there is no agreement since it is never mentioned, but the majority of commentators agree on Mount Tabor.

Mount Tabor is, indeed, a very high mountain and has from the beginning been a special inspiration to Jesus. From Nazareth Mount Tabor is clearly visible and must have spoken volumes to Jesus during his years of growing up. It rises gently, in a well-rounded fashion, from the floor of the great Valley of Esdraelon, just north of Nain, where Jesus raised to life again, out of pure compassion, the only son of a widow.

One can ascend halfway by bus, then take a taxi the rest of the way up Mount Tabor, and when one reaches the top one begins to sense the height and how commanding is the view of the surrounding area. Behind the ruins of an earlier basilica, one is immediately confronted by the present-day basilica, the work of the great Italian architect Barluzzi.

The best time to visit Mount Tabor is the late afternoon, when the sun shines gloriously through the back door on to the great mosaic of the transfiguration over the main altar, for then it seems to take place all over again. What a dramatic episode that is! To view Jesus, transfigured before one's eyes, in anticipation of his glorious resurrection! "Lord, it is indeed good for us to be here!"

We now come to the beautiful story of the Transfiguration, which immediately preceded the passion of Christ. For this, Jesus chose his three favorite apostles: Peter, James, and his brother John. Of course, he told them not to reveal anything about it until the Son of Man should rise from the dead. They did not understand what he told them, because they could not at all picture him rising from the dead. They must have promptly forgotten about the Transfiguration and remembered it again only when the impossible had happened, that Jesus should rise from the dead as he had predicted. It was meant to strengthen the apostles against their failure to trust him when he died.

This scene contains, at the same time, remembrances of his baptism, when the Father had declared him his own son, and of the coming Resurrection, when Jesus would appear after having been buried. Hence, it is certainly a key to the whole gospel account. But what about John, who does not have a transfiguration in his Gospel? No, as usual, John has his own way of doing things, namely in his beautiful chapter 12, where Jesus is mulling over the Father's closeness to him.

All becomes clear with the Resurrection of Jesus, which is patently the Transfiguration come true. But what about the two figures, Moses and Elijah, who appear with Jesus and talk with him about his coming passion. Well, besides the usual explanation that Moses gave the covenant and law and Elijah preserved them, I strongly urge the reasoning that in the Old Testament these are the two figures who had mystical experiences of God, in Exodus 33 and 1 Kings 19. These should be reread in this connection.

The Transfiguration is very important in our personal spiritual life. We need to be constantly reminded to "listen to him." When we have done all the reading that our other duties allow, and when we have read our eyes tired of reading, that is precisely when we need to listen to the Lord speaking to us and reminding us that Jesus is our special guide in the spiritual life. We need to listen to him. Even the great St. Teresa of Avila needed to learn this lesson after she had received all her visions. She learned that, in spite of everything, Jesus needs to be listened to because it was he who won our freedom for us, and he is the one through whom we are to come to the Father.

We must, especially, learn the important lesson that, no matter where we are in the spiritual life, we must look to Jesus as our guide. He became human for us, suffered and died for us, and he is the one who can and will show us how to be like him.

Of course, our own openness to the Transfiguration will affect us in various ways, from the stumbling declaration of Peter, to the silent acceptance of James and John, who did not at all understand what was happening before their eyes. So also with us, we must not at all grow restive or impatient. We should be content with the perception of Christ that is given to us according to our state in the spiritual life, but we should always look forward to understanding him better. Remember, he is the one who is responsible for passive contemplation. Without him we can do nothing, as he explains graphically in John 15, the beautiful parable of the true vine and the branches.

### 4. The Journey to Jerusalem

As we can easily see from any of the Synoptic Gospels, right after the Transfiguration, Jesus sets his face for Jerusalem and what awaited him there. In Luke's Gospel, the journey consumes ten whole chapters (9 to 19). On closer examination it becomes evident that this *hodós* ("way") is really a spiritual journey, for it jumps around the place, but it does contain Jesus' lessons about all the things that in Luke's mind combine to make up a Christian on his or her way with Christ and the apostles to the heavenly Jerusalem.

For our setting of this journey to Jerusalem, I will describe places and events which take place geographically in the middle between Nazareth and Galilee. This is Samaria. Who were the Samaritans? They were the people of the Northern Kingdom who were left after the capture of Samaria by Sargon I of Assyria in 721 B.C.E. and who then intermarried with captive people from other lands. Because they were troubled by wild animals, they decided to adopt the Yahwism of the land, but in an heretical fashion. Hence they were shunned by Jews, especially of Judea, as people of mixed race and false beliefs.

In Samaria there are two mountains, Mount Garizim, the sacred mountain of the Samaritans, and Mount Ebal, the mountain of evil. Together, these two mountains form the good and evil of the Covenant. Then we see the Pool of Jacob, on the basement floor of the Greek Orthodox Church, and third, we have the well-kept tomb of Joseph. Truly, here was God, and I knew it not!

Our Scripture quotations for the Journey to Jerusalem according to Luke are copious indeed, everything from chapter 9 to chapter 19, indeed enough to keep us busy the next year. All we need to do is turn to Luke 9 for our studies. In fact, if we confine ourselves to material that is unique to Luke and has been washed and cleaned, we find that our reading embraces the following: a parable between four events involving Samaritans and events of Jericho; teachings on prayer and miscellaneous teachings; teachings on trust, penance, and preparedness; teachings on the right use of material things; and finally, teachings on humility, and renunciation, as well as teachings on divine mercy and human repentance. These were undoubtedly the key teachings of Christianity and deserved to be thus treated by Luke, all continuing the qualities that any good Jew would immediately approve of on first hearing them.

But when would Luke have had the opportunity to listen to these stories? Perhaps during the two years of Paul's imprisonment at Caesaria? Luke could have traveled extensively through Galilee, Samaria, and Judea, gathering stories and then writing them down in his own imaginative style. So let us in our own journey to the heavenly Jerusalem, meditate on the stories and draw lessons from them for our personal life.

Just how can we hope to practice these virtues? Well, the spiritual life is not just a collection of individual virtues. No, it is nothing less than living the life of Christ himself. Look at the lives of the saints. What they had in common is that each of them imitated Christ in a special way. Christ lives his life in each of us, which is different from the way in which he lives in anyone else. The marvelous thing is that, in imitating Jesus and letting him live in us, we end up practicing all the virtues mentioned above.

Of course, God knows better than we how this economy of salvation works. But what is universally true is that the spiritual life begins with humility, gains through purity of all kinds, and reaches perfection through the practice of charity or Christian life. The marvelous thing is that no matter what our progress, we always need humility, purity, and love, in that order. Our great example is that of Mary, our eternal mother, and our faithful mentor in our relations to her divine Son.

## 5. The Last Supper

To conclude this second series of decades, we need to look at what happened to Jesus on the very night he was betrayed and delivered. Jesus first washed the feet of his apostles and taught his followers to do the same. Next he instituted the new and eternal Covenant in his blood. Then they all went to the Garden of Gethsemane to pray, which is the first of the Sorrowful Mysteries.

Clearly, the edifice where Jesus celebrated the Last Supper is of Crusader construction. This being a matter of faith rather than controversy, let us accept it as a Crusader rebuilding of an earlier structure, perhaps even the home of Mark's mother. At any rate the apostles possessed all they needed to enter into the passion with Jesus. So it is in the Passover seder, after giving his apostles a taste of his body and blood, he then takes them on a long tour of what they could expect and how they were expected to act, expecting them to live according to his instructions. The Holy Eucharist was to be their solace and strength, especially when men would turn against them to seek their lives because of their faith.

If this was the house of John Mark's mother, it is easy to see how Mark, a mere teenager at the time, was sent to bed, but being curious, sneaked a look at proceedings. When they left for Gethsemane, he curiously followed and was there for arresting, but instead let go his night clothes and sped away naked.

Whether this was the authentic place of sorrow and peace, it seems to answer well the needs of Scripture, even to the tomb of David being nearby, as is clearly indicated by the cloth over the tomb, which reads, "Ha Melek David."

In this, the last decade of the second series of decades, we come to the richest of references. On this, the last night of Jesus' stay in Jerusalem, we celebrate his Passover, the institution of the Eucharist, the inauguration of the New Covenant, and finally his long farewell discourse.

The institution of the Eucharist occurs in Matthew, Mark, Luke, and in 1 Corinthians 11. What is remarkable about the institution of the Eucharist is that, in all the places where it is mentioned in the New Testament, the verbs are always in the present tense. In other words, it seems evident that, in the words of Jesus, the sacrifice is taking place then and there, without having to wait until the next day at Mount Calvary.

That this is also the inauguration of a New Covenant is also clear from the words used. In every instance of the institution of the Eucharist, it is evident that it is a Covenant Sacrifice. The Covenant was the most important idea in the divine-human relationship. A covenant was an agreement establishing a relationship between two people or peoples, and it is evident from the wording of the Sinai Covenant that this was the most important concept, before the law, which is not given until the following chapter.

John's Gospel does not give the institution of the Eucharist, but in Jesus' long farewell discourse there is much material covered. Even just a casual reading of the discourse material in John's Gospel is sufficient to give us a great deal to think about. "Whoever loves me will keep my word, and my Father will love him, and we will come to him and make our dwelling with him" (14:23). How consoling those words, and how well they fit in with the institution of the Eucharist.

As we come to the reflection on the Passover and the accompanying sermon, how much is there to think about? Jesus gives himself to us under the lowly forms of bread and wine, that he may more easily transform us into himself. The Church has very wisely surrounded the words of institution with vestments, prayers, and actions calculated to teach us about the Eucharist (thanksgiving), about the Covenant, about the Farewell Address of Jesus. If she had left it as Jesus spoke it, it would have lasted just about one minute, and most Catholics would miss the Eucharist, but she has put it in the drama of the Liturgy of the Word and of the Eucharist, so that we might more fully participate and appreciate. And when we realize that the main offering is that of ourselves in union with Jesus, this motivation gives us reason for giving ourselves wholeheartedly in the sacrifice. The Church makes this clear by quoting from the prayer of Azarias in the book of Daniel, chapter 3. The three young men, thrown into the fire because they refused to worship a false God, had nothing to offer, so they offered themselves and begged to be received as whole-burnt offerings.

The long farewell discourse of Jesus gives us additional thoughts to be pondered. What is the purpose of all this? To be perfectly bound to him. Just as nutritionists tell us that we become what we eat and drink, so it is with this. The realization that Jesus is always with us, to strengthen us, to change us into himself, to show his love for us, these and other considerations almost overwhelm us with their profundity.

# The Sorrowful Mysteries

### 1. The Agony in the Garden

Having completed the Passover celebration and inaugurated a New Covenant in his blood as he instituted the Holy Eucharist, and having addressed his followers in the most tender terms, Jesus was now ready to begin his Passion with the most heart-rending prayer ever prayed which ended indeed with "thy will be done."

The place was called Gethsemane, which means "Olive Press," and it rested at the foot of the Mount of Olives. While there are several trees that may be old enough to date back to Christ, four in particular seem old, rough, and ample enough to fill the bill. But besides the trees themselves, part of the garden has been set aside for prayer, and when entering this church, a person is filled with a sense of Jesus' prayer and agony in the garden.

First, it is especially striking that all the windows are of a deep purple. In the front a large stone is set off from the rest of the church by a crown of thorns made of iron. The enclosed stone would make the ideal place for Jesus to repose himself full length in prayer.

The entire place of prayer and agony is so conducive to prayer, even an agonizing prayer, that the natural inclination is to remain there silently praying and agonizing in union with Jesus. Let it never be forgotten that this prayer, though said in a garden, was still higher and more effective than the transfiguration prayer, which was said on a mountain top. Through a quirk of nature, the fact is that the Jerusalem massive is higher than the single top of Tabor.

The Scriptures concerning Jesus' prayer and agony are brief. It seems that the evangelists did not want to draw out Jesus suffering, albeit that they understood it fully from their personal observation. Jesus, of course, did not take his whole band of apostles with him but rather just the same three who had witnessed his transfiguration. Then, leaving them at a certain spot, he went on a little farther, and immediately began his beautiful prayer, "Father, if it is possible, let this cup pass from me; yet, not as I will but as you will" (Matt 26:39; Mark 14:36; Luke 22:42).

He prayed thus three times, emphasizing and reemphasizing the importance of his prayer and checking on the apostles in the meantime, but finding them asleep, he chided them for not being able to watch one hour with him. They promptly went back to sleep, so little was their appreciation of his prayer.

The part in Luke's Gospel about an angel coming to him and about his sweat being like blood flowing from his body does not seem to possess the same claim to authenticity as the more familiar texts, but those texts give us the picture well enough of Jesus' prayer and agony in the garden.

Jesus was human, and as such, he prayed to be spared of his anticipated suffering, but nevertheless, he was always willing to accept whatever the Father willed, even if it meant the extreme of pain and death.

The application of Jesus' prayer and agony in the garden to our own lives is most important. Frequently in our lifetime we are faced with a dilemma in which the two alternatives from which we must choose are not attractive to us. We would like to avoid both of them, but we cannot. That is precisely when we must pray, and pray we will, like Jesus, if we are people of prayer.

Note, especially in Luke's Gospel, that Jesus was a deeply prayerful person. He prayed quite naturally at every important step in his life and career. Prayer was indeed his communication with God, with whom he was in such deep mystical relationship that the most natural thing for him any time was to pray. He prayed when he was filled with joy and when he was filled with sadness. It was the most natural thing for him to do, and it should be the most natural thing for us as well.

We have a tendency to value prayer according to how it makes us feel. Thus we think of Jesus' prayer when he was transfigured as being the most perfect kind. But such is not the case. No, it is when we pray in the midst of our sad times, our agonies, that we pray most perfectly. And here nature helps us because Jesus prayed in the garden, where on account of the height of Jerusalem's massive, it was the most perfect of all his prayers, even greater than at Mount Tabor, which was high, but in comparison with the surrounding valley, not equally above sea level.

## 2. The Scourging at the Pillar

After his prayer and agony in the Garden of Gethsemane, Jesus was arrested and taken across the Kidron Valley, up a flight of steps which is still very visible, to the House of Caiphas, marked now by the Church of Galli Cantu. There are a number of underground rooms, in one of which Jesus was kept overnight, subject to periodic beatings and spittle. Then, in the morning, he was taken to the Praetorium, the official residence of Pontius Pilate just north of the Temple area. Here, he was subjected to the scourging, crowning with thorns, individual tortures, so that he truly became "a worm, hardly human" (Ps 22:7).

Today, we wind our way up the outside road from the Church of the Prayer and Agony in the Garden through the Gate of St. Stephen, along the street of St. Francis, until we come to the Convent of Notre Dame du Sion. These sisters were founded by Alphonse Ratisbonne, who was converted from Judaism to Christianity by a vision of Mary in the Church of the Fratti in Rome.

Entering here, we wait a while and then are taken downstairs where we can walk on the very stones of the Praetorium, the same stones made sacred by the blood of Christ. Here in the stones we can see the games of the King, which were carved there from the time of Jesus himself.

In this most sacred spot, walking on the very same stones on which Jesus walked, we are filled with awe. It was here that Jesus was revealed for who he was, true God become man to save us from our sins. It was here that he endured the terrible unlimited scourging, which in its ferocity went far beyond preparation for crucifixion. And why? This scourging was especially for our sins of the flesh. Jesus, mercy!

Scripture is not very informative about the scourging of Jesus, but we know about it from historical records and also from the Holy Shroud of Turin. I include the shroud because it seems to me that the tests which have been publicized about it, placing it in the Middle Ages, leave several things to be desired (e.g., the fact that the image on the cloth is a scorch which acts as a photographic negative, long before photography was invented).

What we know from these other sources is that, unlike Jewish scourging, which did not exceed forty stripes, the Roman scourging was unlimited. It was usually administered by two soldiers, each of whom held in his hand two strips of leather with a little device of iron or bone to sink into the flesh. From the Holy Shroud of Turin, it is evident that the two scourgers of Jesus must have delivered about two hundred blows before they tired of their task and called it a day, leaving Jesus attached to the pillar in a pool of blood.

In Jerusalem, in the Church of the Holy Sepulchre, there is a small pillar which purports to be the pillar of the scourging. Whether it is authentic or not, I cannot say, but at least it gives us some idea of what the pillar looked like. On the Holy

Shroud it is obvious that Jesus must have suffered about two hundred scourges, more or less, because his entire body front and back is covered with stripes, which must have been very painful when his clothes were put back on.

Let us now just contemplate the scourging in all its reality. It is obvious that the evangelists cringed from describing its intensity in detail, simply stating the fact and leaving it to the reader to fill in the details.

What does the scourging of Jesus mean to us? What to me in particular? It seems to me that Jesus underwent the scourging to atone for our sins of self-indulgence or downright sinfulness regarding the body. This is one of the most common sins, one that is especially characteristic of human beings because we have a body, which is a source of temptations for most of our life.

Let us, as we contemplate the scourging of Jesus, dwell on its purpose, namely, to atone for our sins of the flesh, which include more than the body. If we examine the sins of the flesh in Galatians 5 and Romans 8, we see that it includes more than sins of the body. This is our whole person, body and soul, in all our human weakness, subject to temptations and sins, to illness and accident, to death. Let us freely acknowledge our humanness and deplore our sins of the flesh, which caused such great suffering for the very Son of God.

And when one considers the sinfulness of humankind as a whole through all the centuries since, what a burden of sin there was for Jesus to atone for, and for us to join him in this suffering, the scourging. Perhaps we do not now undergo any painful diseases, but sooner or later the time will come when we have to. Let it be suffering on our part in union with Jesus for our fellow humans. "In my flesh I am filling up what is lacking in the afflictions of Christ on behalf of his body, which is the church" (Col 1:24).

## 3. The Crowning with Thorns

After the scourging, limited only by the endurance of the scourgers, it would seem that Jesus had reached the limit of suffering, but no! In addition to the ordinary suffering of the scourging preceding a crucifixion, the soldiers had devised a particularly devilish torture uniquely for their captive. We know of no other prisoner anywhere who was crowned with thorns as Jesus was. Not just the tiny little rose thorns in a circlet around his head, as we often see in paintings, but the long acacia (honey locust) thorns woven into a cap and then pressed down into his entire head, some even piercing through his forehead. How ironic! This was the king of the Jews? Good! Then, let us make sport of him and crown him with these cruel thorns!

To honor the crowning with thorns, we have gone next door to the Sisters of Notre Dame du Sion. We are still walking on the very stones of the Pretorium, such was its extension, but in a different spot, below the chapel of the Franciscans, down in their basement, where we look up and see, circling over our heads, the unmistakable cruelty of the crown of thorns.

Why this extreme of cruelty? Would not the scourging have been enough? For any of us, of course, but not for the suffering servant of YHWH. If he suffered the cruel scourging for our sins of the flesh, he wanted just as badly to suffer the terrible crowning with thorns for our sins of the soul, sins not involving the body, such as pride, covetousness, anger, hatred, envy, and all the other sins we drink down daily without giving them a thought. O Jesus, let me learn from your crown of thorns to avoid the greater sins of the soul.

The Scriptures give a few more details regarding the crowning with thorns, but they fail to tell us what kind of thorns are spoken of, and so medieval artists have drilled into our minds a picture of rose thorns wound around in a circlet and placed gingerly on Jesus' head. The truth, as we see from the Holy Shroud of Turin, is that it was the honey-locust that provided the thorns, some three to five inches long, that formed a cap on Jesus' head. In fact, again from the shroud, it is evident that at least one of those thorns pierced through the forehead of Jesus, causing a stream of blood to flow from the wound.

Such was the suffering in the crowning with thorns, but what was the purpose of it? Well, that seems to have been determined by one of the games noted in the stones of the house of the Sisters of Notre Dame de Sion, called the *Saturnalia*. This was a game in which a prisoner was dressed like a king and then mocked. This is exactly what happened in Jesus' case. After the thorns were placed on his head, he was mocked as a false king, struck on the head, and the thorns driven in farther. Meanwhile, Jesus was challenged to declare who had struck him.

What a cruel torture was this! The physical pain of the crowning was one thing, but the cruel mockery of Jesus as king must have been especially tortuous to Jesus, who indeed was not only a king, but the king of kings, even the God of these torturers.

We know of no other crowning with thorns. It seems logical that they would have practiced this farce with some others besides Jesus, given that there is in the very stones the game of *Saturnalia*. But as a matter of fact, we do not know of a single instance of this.

What kind of sins did Jesus atone for in the crowning with thorns? Our monstrous sins of pride. Being humans, we think that our greatest sins are those of the flesh, but such is not the case. Look at the New Testament. Jesus condemns, of course, our sins of the flesh, but these are regarded as characteristic of humans. But sins of pride, these are regarded as attacks on the deity himself. Hence, it is clearly regarded time and time again as the principal sin of human beings, and, for that matter, of angels.

Could we see ourselves as God sees us, how could we possibly be guilty of pride? All that is good in us is from God, not from ourselves. All we can claim as our own are our sins, and if we are proud of those we are in a sad state indeed.

That is why humility, the realization of what we are of ourselves, is the foundation of the whole spiritual life. No matter what other virtues we have, if we haven't got humility, we have nothing. We must turn to God for everything in this life, especially the spiritual gifts. We can see how Jesus was really atoning for our monstrous pride when he endured the painful crowning with thorns.

In this, as in the previous atonement, we should regard not only our own sins, but those of the human race, from Jesus' time until now. What a travesty through the centuries, one human being after another raising himself up as if he had done anything of which he could brag. Let us humble ourselves as human beings, in order to win the approval of God and to atone for the sins of pride on the part of our human race.

## 4. The Carrying of the Cross

After my descriptions of the scourging at the pillar and the crowning with thorns, we are then expected to figure out how it was possible for Jesus to put forth the energy to find the way of the cross from the Pretorium to the Church of the Holy Sepulchre, all the while carrying the heavy crossbeam of the cross. What an effort it must have been on his part, even with the help of Simon the Cyrenean, to make even a single step, let alone some seven hundred.

For today the distance of the Via Dolorosa is about seven hundred yards, more or less, and we must remember that in Jesus' day, it measured more because of the descent into the Tyropoeon Valley and up again on the other side. Besides, the way led through the active way of the buyers and sellers of Jerusalem, who must have resented this intrusion on their livelihood.

From time immemorial Christians have been able to endure the Way of the Cross by following the fourteen stations specified by the Franciscans. Many of them are authentic, but just as many are not. More recently, for example in the Cathedral of the Madeleine at Salt Lake City, the scriptural fourteen stations rather than the traditional legendary ones are offered. Whichever ones are meditated on, let it be done with all sincerity, truly putting oneself in the place of Jesus and suffering the torment of his Way of the Cross.

Why did he choose to undergo this torment? Was it not to give us the example that "If anyone wishes to come after me, he must deny himself and take up his cross daily and follow me" (Luke 9:23). Jesus preached no "cry-baby Christianity."

What are the Scripture passages dealing with Jesus' carrying the cross to Calvary? Very few indeed. Practically all the evangelists tell us is that Jesus, carrying his own cross, went to the place of execution and also that the soldiers picked Simon the Cyrenean to carry the cross, obviously because it was evident that Jesus, after his scourging and crowning with thorns, was close to death and incapable of carrying the cross all the way to Calvary.

This is the Via Dolorosa, the Sorrowful Way of the Cross, which the good Franciscans have offered the world in fourteen stations so that anyone could, by this means, be able to follow Christ in the Way of the Cross. But unfortunately the stations can contain some which are apocryphal, such as the wiping of the face of Jesus on the cloth of Veronica, whose name (in Latin and Greek) means "True Image." It has been discovered in recent years that the image of Veronica is a direct copy of the face of Jesus on the shroud.

Some scripturists, of course, keep those stations which are mentioned in the Bible and add others which are also authentic, dropping only those which are not mentioned in the Bible. This is admirable and has been copied in the recent restoration of the Cathedral of the Madeleine.

In Luke's Gospel, Jesus at least addresses himself to the women of Jerusalem, who are weeping over him. He tells them not to, for if these things are done to the green wood, what will be done to the dry? So Jesus advises the weeping women to weep for themselves and their fellow citizens because of the coming suffering when Jerusalem will be destroyed by the Romans in the year A.D. 70.

Where does Jesus' carrying of his cross fit into our lives? Did not Jesus say, more than once, "Whoever wishes to come after me must deny himself, take up his cross, and follow me" (Mark 8:34). So Jesus obviously invites us, no, he demands of us, that we follow him carrying our cross on the way to Calvary.

In other words, Jesus invites us to participate in his sorrowful Way of the Cross. In Lent, we have the common practice of saying the stations, either publicly or privately. This is admirable because it involves the kind of personal prayer, meditation, or contemplation that are so important in the spiritual life.

This is our principal lesson, namely, to unite ourselves with Christ as he carries his cross to Calvary. This means through our whole lives, and in every circumstance of our lives, we are to imitate Jesus by following him, without murmuring, on the road to Calvary.

But remember that Jesus had to carry his cross right through the busy crowd and streets without being distracted by the commotion of business going on all about him. And we must do the same. A word about Simon the Cyrenean, whom the soldiers chose to carry the crossbeam for Jesus: he must have become a Christian because he is mentioned by Mark in Rome as being the father of Alexander and Rufus, who were obviously well known to the Christians of Rome.

## 5. The Crucifixion of Jesus

The terminus of the Via Dolorosa is the church of the tomb of Christ. As churches go, it is one of the oldest, most composite, and least beautiful. But, fortunately, one does not visit the Church of the Holy Sepulchre in search of beauty. No, one goes there in order to savor its history, and history is there aplenty.

First, there we find stations ten, eleven, twelve, thirteen, and fourteen, but a sharp distinction is made. At the heart of the church stands the empty tomb of Jesus (station fourteen) and not too far from that is the place of the enshrouding (station thirteen). The three previous stations are in a side chapel, to which one climbs by a stone staircase of some twenty steps. Station ten, where Jesus is stripped of his garments, is beautifully portrayed in a mosaic along the right wall of this chapel. On the back wall and to the right is station eleven (the Crucifixion), while in between is a small altar of the Stabat Mater or Sorrowful Mother. And finally to the left there is the Greek Orthodox Chapel of the Crucifixion or death of Jesus on the cross. And here at this altar is a circle below the altar where pilgrims may stretch out their hands, touch the ground of the hill, and acknowledge the great love with which Jesus gave his life for us.

Let us leave the empty tomb for a later discussion and turn to the agony of Jesus' death by crucifixion. From time to time we feel a deep sense of sorrow over Jesus' death for us, while at the same time a deep sense of gratitude over the kind of death he bore for us, so that no one will ever surpass his love for us.

According to Scripture Jesus was nailed to the cross where he died. The Greek Orthodox altar, with its multitude of lamps, marks the site of the Crucifixion. Below the altar is the opening to the mountain where a person can touch the very ground which bore Jesus up. All of this is within the Church of the Holy Sepulchre, where we celebrate his death as well as his resurrection.

But the most important Scripture references, it seems to me, are those containing Jesus' final seven words. For example, while being nailed to the cross, he said, "Father, forgive them, they know not what they do" (Luke 23:34). Next, he gave his dear mother to John's care, a clear indication that he was an only Son. He called out, *"Eloi, Eloi, lema sabachthani"* (Mark 15:34), a quotation which forms the opening of Psalm 21, but also represents his desolation of spirit. When the good thief defended him and asked for a place in his kingdom, he said, "Today you will be with me in Paradise" (Luke 23:43). Then he called out, "I thirst," and finally, "It is finished" (John 19:30). He said all the right things from his pulpit, the cross.

In addition, Scripture adds that at the cross were Mary, his Mother, John the Evangelist, and Mary Magdalene. These three had endured everything with Jesus before, and now they would live out his dying. These are the final words of Jesus to us, and there is a world of meaning in them.

So let us be silent while we contemplate Jesus' death on the cross or in his Blessed Mother's arms when he is taken down, and let us meditate on Jesus who has given his life so that we may live. God has died for us his creatures, and sinful creatures at that!

What caused Jesus' death on the cross? Was it the punishment that he had endured from the scourging and the crowning? Was it his loss of blood from the nailing of his wrists and feet to the cross? Or was it from a combination of these things? From medical investigations, it seems that what took his life on the cross was the inability to keep pushing himself up from his feet to be able to breathe, so it was basically from asphyxiation. After about three hours of pushing himself up, it became impossible. Jesus simply said, "It is finished" (John 19:30) and died for us.

And then, since Pilate was not sure of Jesus' death, he had a soldier pierce his side with a lance, and there emerged blood and water. It has been suggested that these were the signs of a broken heart, but whether that be true of Jesus or not, is not quite clear. Symbolically, it certainly is true that the Church and the sacraments represented by the blood and water were born of Jesus crucified.

In the Church of the Holy Sepulchre, a short pace from the Chapel of the Crucifixion, there is the place of the anointing of the body, which also commemorates the Holy Shroud of Turin. Since it was a holy day, it was necessary to bury the body quickly, with a minimum of anointing, so they quickly anointed the body and placed it in the tomb of Joseph of Arimathea, which was at Calvary. All these sites are in the Church of the Holy Sepulchre in the vicinity of the Crucifixion. We will get back to the tomb when we take the next mystery, that of the Resurrection.

Now we wait silently through Saturday, with the tomb guarded by a detachment of soldiers, while Jesus is preparing for his Resurrection the next day. Let us keep guard with him.

# The Glorious Mysteries

### 1. The Resurrection of Jesus

For this first of the Glorious Mysteries, our attention is drawn to the central point of the Church of the Holy Sepulchre, the empty tomb. Now sadly at the very heart of Christianity, we must deal with the fact of division amongst us. The tomb not only stands as the most important place in the Church, but it is divided: half devoted to Latin Catholicism, half to the other believers, particularly the Greek Orthodox. Be that as it may, there is still much room for all who believe to honor their faith.

The first thing that greets the eye when one enters the Latin Catholics' portion of the tomb is an alabaster stand that seems to hold a special fascination, and with good reason, for it contains a portion of the huge stone that was at the entrance to the tomb. Whether this is authentically part of the stone that covered Jesus' tomb is not quite as certain, but it does not make all that much difference. Then we enter the tomb proper.

The tomb accommodates only one or two persons at a time, so one is prepared to venerate the sight, with its inscriptions and tokens of honor, but what speaks to us most of all is that the slab on which the body rested is now totally empty and clean. He is not here. Where is he then? In heaven, in the Eucharist, in the Scriptures, in each of us by grace, in the whole body of the faithful, etc. He is more with us than in his lifetime!

Jesus, risen from the dead for our justification and salvation, remain with us and help us see you in all the ways you are with us. Go before us as we continue to strive to overcome the world, the flesh, and the devil. Oh, may our faith, hope, and love be strong in you.

The great surprise about the actual Gospels was the Resurrection. Evidently, this was a surprise for the whole world. Why? Because no one expected someone who died to rise again from the dead on the third day. If Jesus had spoken about rising from the dead, this would be a great miracle, unintelligible to anyone hearing it. Hence, the apostles did not at all expect it.

How was this honestly different from Christmas? At Christmas Jesus is born into our human race, whereas in the Resurrection, which is probably the greatest feast in the whole Church, he is reborn as a life-giving spirit.

But the Resurrection of Jesus was unique in history. It was a resurrection. There has never been, before or since, such a resurrection. It meant that Jesus could use human functions if he wished, but he did not have to. He could eat and sleep if he wished to, but he did not need to. He ate with his disciples, he walked with them, but he did not need to. His body had taken on all the faculties belonging to the soul.

Moreover, as to his face, apparently there was a certain glow about it that if one did not realize this, then Jesus was unrecognized. But how in the world would one have had a similar experience before Jesus rose from the dead. He would not, but nevertheless he can and should be experienced by the apostles, and then he is recognized as he is.

O Jesus, let me so experience you in my prayer, that my powers may be able to recognize you when my own time comes. You are risen from the dead and remain always with us in your risen state. You are the one who gives life to all of us until the end of time.

How do we apply the Resurrection to our daily lives? Not easily. We must remember that it is precisely as newly risen that he was first known by his beloved apostles. And as such, many did not recognize him.

Easter differs from Christmas in that we have had the experience of seeing newborn children. We not only see them but our heart goes out to them. That is what we celebrate at Christmas: Jesus being born like us. And so it is easy for us to celebrate, to penetrate the mystery. At Easter, however, we are celebrating a risen man in a glorious resurrection, for which we have no experience. That is why we have so many different figures signifying life, such as an egg or a rabbit. I like the figure of a butterfly myself. The insect is first a caterpillar, then a chrysalis, then a butterfly. And there is all the difference in the world between the caterpillar and the butterfly. Butterflies are free, without any restraints, such as a caterpillar has, moving so slowly across the face of a branch or leaf.

During the Easter season, we rightly make much of flowers. After all, this is spring, and flowers are expected—and very appropriate! There will be only as many fruit in the harvest as there were flowers in the spring. So, let us celebrate with flowers in abundance, all kinds of flowers and as many blooms of each kind as we can afford. This will begin to portray the meaning of the Resurrection of Jesus for us. He is risen in flowers, which will fall off, and then in their place we will come to see the glorious Resurrection of Jesus for us.

Dear Jesus, risen immortally and glorious, I see you in the midst of the flowers of our generation, so that I may be able to recognize you as the newly and gloriously risen Son of God.

## 2. The Ascension of Jesus to Heaven

Forty days after he arose from the dead and rejoined his apostles, Jesus ascended into heaven, thus enlightening them and strengthening them for their tremendous task ahead. This was something that needed to be done gradually, so that after several issues of progress and positive thinking the apostolic Church would be ready for its great task ahead.

In the meantime, the apostles were the objects of the curious who needed to know whether they had crossed the threshold and experienced spiritual things in a way that surpassed everything extraordinary. And what about now? Did they have the privilege of so seeing things that it was as if there were no other truths than that of Christ?

Actually, accounts of the Ascension event are found only in Luke's Gospel and Acts, which means that it pales in importance to the Resurrection account, which is described abundantly in every Gospel as well as in the principal addresses in Acts. And correspondingly the event of the Ascension is preserved by only two structures, the Greek Orthodox Church of the Ascension and the little Orthodox eight-sided chapel, which purportedly contained the last footprint on earth of the Messiah himself.

The lesson of the Ascension was clear to the apostles and to all us Christian believers: If the Christ had remained with us, we would never have received the Holy Spirit. But rather let us part with the consolation of his presence with us in favor of his presence in a different way. We have a great task ahead of us, and we have no time to lose in fulfilling it with the help of the Holy Spirit and with the strong backing of Christ himself. Let us love and work.

What do the Scriptures tell us about the Ascension of Jesus? Actually, very little, and that only in the writings of Luke, that is in the last page of the Gospel and in the first page of the Acts, and even here the Ascension is so described that it marks the conclusion of the forty days of being with his apostles and instructing them for their task of evangelization.

But are there not some details in each account of Luke's that we can use for our own instruction? Yes, there are. For example, in Luke's Gospel, Jesus suddenly appeared in their midst and, to their incredulous minds, he argued that he was no ghost and even ate a piece of dried fish in their presence. Then, he reminded them that he had said that all the Scriptures, from the time of Moses onward, had to be fulfilled, and he opened their minds to understand the Scriptures. He told them to stay in Jerusalem until the coming of the Holy Spirit, who would be with them in their task of evangelization, and then, while still speaking with them, he blessed them and ascended to heaven. The apostles, overcome with the grief of his leaving them, were daily praying in the Temple.

In the account of the Ascension in Acts 1:6-11, they are going to the Mount of Olives, and Jesus is asked if he would establish the kingdom of Israel at this time, to which he responds that it is not for them to know these things, but that they are to remain in Jerusalem awaiting the coming of the Holy Spirit through whom they would preach in Jerusalem, Judea, Samaria, and to the ends of the earth. Then he was lifted up before their eyes, and two angels appeared to warn them against looking up to heaven because he would return to them in the same way that he had left them.

What lessons does the Ascension possess for us, the followers of Jesus? From the structure of the act and from the foregoing Scriptures, we find many lessons.

First, there is the primary lesson that with the Ascension of Jesus into heaven, our flesh is to be seated at the right hand of the Father. What dignity does our human nature take on? This mortal nature, which so suffered on the cross for us will now be in triumph at the right hand of God. The more we contemplate this fact, the more we come to recognize the great call of our humanity and how much we are called to live saintly lives in this world so that we can be the more prepared to live close to God in the future.

Moreover, there is much that we can learn from the last sayings of Jesus to us. First, that we must try to understand the Scriptures that concern him, from Moses and all the prophets, so that we can appreciate him. And just as Jesus himself opened his apostles' minds to understand the Scriptures concerning him, so we too can count on him as our teacher to open our minds and understand the Scriptures.

Finally, we should learn from Jesus' farewell words and the words of the two angels, namely that our task is to evangelize the poor. In this task Jesus will help us, and so will the Holy Spirit, whom we will receive anew in the next mystery. With these we are quite capable of spreading Jesus' Gospel throughout the world.

## 3. The Descent of the Holy Spirit

After the events of Holy Thursday evening, some scholars have wondered whether the large so-called Upper Room where Jesus and the apostles were to eat the Passover could be the home of Mark's mother. She was hosting the whole Christian community gathered in prayer in Acts 12, when Peter was miraculously freed from prison. This would explain the "man carrying a water jug" and the mysterious streaker in the garden as Mark himself, for both stories are found only in Mark's Gospel.

As we have already seen in the final aspect of Jesus' life in the last of the Fruitful Mysteries, the Church of the Institution of the Eucharist has had a very colorful career. What we now have is a Crusader structure of more than one level, which has been used as a church, then turned into a mosque, and is now a kind of museum. It was here that the Christians gathered in prayer (the first novena of prayer) after Jesus' Ascension. Altogether, the Christian community formed about one hundred and twenty persons (enough to start a community among the Jews), including Mary, the Blessed Mother of Jesus. Suddenly, there was a great wind (*pneûma* means "wind" as well as "spirit"), and there appeared tongues of flame, which separated and rested on each one of them, so that they began to speak in foreign languages under the guidance of the Holy Spirit. This was Pentecost! This was the baptism and consecration of the early Church!

Dear Jesus, open my mind to receive the Holy Spirit. Help me to realize that, without him, I am not yet truly Christian. Help me to understand that the Holy Spirit is entrusted with the task of transforming me into Jesus and of introducing me to the Holy Trinity.

What do the Scriptures have to say about our Pentecost? Not a great deal, and yet just about enough to aid us on this task. First of all, there were one hundred and twenty people in all, including the Mother of Jesus, and they were enough to form a community with its own rabbi among the Jewish people.

Where were they gathered? The Scriptures do not say exactly, but as we have already seen, the place could easily have been the home of Mark's mother, where the entire Church will gather in chapter 12, awaiting the disposition of Peter to them.

First came a mighty wind, then tongues of flame, one over each head, signifying that they all participated in this coming, and remember that the Holy Spirit came upon them in a special way. They received each a flame, each a language never taught to them, so that it was evident to the Jews that something extraordinary was going on. In fact, the apostles were even accused of being drunk with wine. Peter, rising up, first rejected the drunken idea, and then he explained that they had received the Holy Spirit, which enabled them to understand a lot of things.

Then, he quoted David speaking in the psalms and referred to the end times. These were not spoken of themselves, for they had news of David's life and death and, in fact, his tomb was within easy reach. But rather, he looked ahead to the coming of Christ, who had done marvelous deeds among them, been put to death, but God has raised him from the dead, something unheard of throughout the history of the world.

Now all of them had seen and conversed with the risen Christ and could vouch for him. Repent and receive baptism for forgiveness.

And what about us? Is there no lesson which we can gain for ourselves, so that our lives may be useful for the spreading of the kingdom of God? Believe, receive the baptism of the New Covenant, and you shall be saved and belong to the Church of Jesus Christ, so that you may be able to preach Christ from personal knowledge and zeal. About three thousand people were added to the Church that first day.

He, Jesus, has chosen a band of twelve men who, together with their associates, were to go over the whole earth and preach the Gospel to every nation and every creature. This seems to be an impossible task, but let us not forget his promise to us that we would become spiritual beings, for the evangelization of the world. "This is bound to succeed, with us or without us, it is up to us." If we pay close mind and let ourselves become real possessors and participants in Christ himself, then there is no reason whatsoever to hold ourselves back from going forward with Jesus. Moreover, this is around the time of the Purim, the Jewish feast characterized by the wearing of costumes, somewhat like our Mardi Gras. But for us, the lesson is real, namely that as a member of the clergy of the Church of Christ, I must use my opportunities to grow in Christ, and let him grow in us to the fullness of his age, so that we will be ready for the fullness of the harvest and act and preach like him. The thought of all this is almost overwhelming for me, in the sense that, as Christ, I am called to make myself a perfect image of the Almighty.

## 4. The Assumption of Mary

In honoring the blessed Assumption of Mary, the Mother of God, we have three places to consider. The first is the Church of the Dormition of Mary at Jerusalem. This has been the traditional setting of her dormition or sleep in death from about the time of the Council of Ephesus, A.D. 431. It is a very beautiful church, featuring the supine statue of Mary as she would have been venerated in her death. This church is, along with the Upper Room or Cenacle, the crowning point of what is now known as "Sion" or "Zion."

The second place is a beautiful Greek Orthodox Tomb of Mary, which is at one end of the Garden of Gethsemane. It is, of course, far below the tomb of Jesus at the Church of the Holy Sepulchre, but it does show the gentle reverence that the Orthodox followers of Christ have always exhibited toward Mary. They are equal to Latin Catholics in their use of images of Mary, but with one very important distinction, namely they always show her holding the Christ Child as a symbol that all of Mary's great honor, dignity, and reverence are due entirely to her divine Son.

The third place is outside of Ephesus, where the House of the Virgin is found and venerated. Anne Catherine Emmerich (1773–1834) is the principal source of this knowledge. In her *The Life of the Blessed Virgin Mary* she describes in detail Mary's life, death, and assumption outside of Ephesus, and all this has been confirmed in more recent times by the discovery by two young Vincentian priests of the flooring of a structure that corresponds exactly to the description of Catherine Emmerich. The house has been restored, and a healing source of water discovered. Pope Paul VI visited and blessed it.

What do the Scriptures have to say about the Assumption of Mary? Directly, not a single thing. The study of the Assumption, like that of Mary's parents, Joachim and Anne, is based entirely on apocryphal literature, but it is very old literature and seems to reflect the actual fact.

It was the Council of Ephesus in A.D. 431 that gives us the background for the Feast of the Assumption. Mind you, at that time the Church did not venerate any place not made sacred by the life or death of the person honored. The very fact, then, that the Council was held at Ephesus and declared that Mary was *Theotokos,* that is, the Mother of God, is very significant. All of Mary's other privileges flow from the basic fact that she is the Mother of God, not the Trinity, not the Creator, but the Mother of God, because she gives birth to a person and that person is the Son of God and Redeemer of the world.

This has been somewhat substantiated in modern times by the discovery at Ephesus of the house made sacred by Mary and John until her Assumption into heaven. And the many pilgrimages centering on the house at Ephesus are additional support to the proposition that Mary was indeed assumed into heaven, most likely at Ephesus.

Let us then, as we pray the Rosary, be silent and venerate her great dignity and the fact that we can call her indeed *Theótokos,* Mother of God.

What application does this mystery have to our daily life? The application that, when all is said and done, Mary is indeed the refuge of sinners, the help of Christians, the Mother of God. Indeed it is the first chapter of Luke's Gospel with the three-fold story of the Annunciation and Mary's response, as well as the two following mysteries of the Visitation and the Birth of Jesus, that gives us all the material we need to meditate on in connection with the Assumption of Mary.

To recall to the mind those three Mysteries, let me remind the reader that, in the first Mystery we have the three-fold annunciation of the angel Gabriel that Mary is to be the Mother of Jesus, who will be called and will be the Son of God. Then we have Mary's response: at first, a silent one of humility, then her spoken response of purity, and finally her complete loving surrender to God, "Behold, I am the handmaid of the Lord. May it be done to me according to your word."

In the following mystery, that of the Visitation, we have a beautiful example not only of practical love on Mary's part but also her dignity in parallel with the ark of the covenant, which is the main feature of the story in 2 Samuel 6, with which the story of the Visitation is linked, especially with the saying, "Who am I that the Mother of my Lord should come to me?"

In the third Mystery, the Birth of Jesus, we see the actual living out of the mystery, whereby Mary gives birth to the son and places him in the manger. The next two mysteries also add something to our contemplation, in the prophecies of Simeon and in the finding of Jesus in the Temple and his going back with Mary and Joseph to Nazareth and being obedient to them until his baptism.

## 5. The Queenship of Mary

In the last decade of our Rosary, when we finally take a good look at Mary and acknowledge her as Queen of Angels and Men and Women, it is a good time to examine anew just how and in how many ways she has been honored by God as the Mother of her son, yes, and our mother and help, particularly in the shadows of our life. One of the most effective ways of doing this is to look at several of the apparitions with which she has favored our civilization lately.

The first apparition in modern times is that of Rue de Bac, the motherhouse of the Daughters of Charity of St. Vincent de Paul. In four apparitions St. Catherine Laboure was given the design of the Miraculous Medal, which was not a statue but an introduction to the Immaculate Conception, which would be declared a dogma in 1854, just twenty-four years after the apparitions of 1830. Surprisingly, this many years later, St. Catherine's body is still preserved.

The second is Lourdes which is a wonderful confirmation of the correctness of the dogma of the Immaculate Conception in 1854. Lourdes is at once the confirmation of the dogma five years later and a perpetual source of Mary's motherly love for us all.

The third appearance of Mary is that of Fatima in 1917, with its prophecy about World War II, about the conversion of Russia, and the secret prophecy intended for the pope in 1960, and finally the miracle of the sun before thousands of people. And every month, on the thirteenth, crowds come from all over to honor Mary.

Our fourth and final appearance is that of Medjugorje, which occurred in 1981, and amazingly, has taken place almost every day since. This, Mary has declared, is her last appearance in time.

This Feast of the Queenship of Mary brings to my memory a very special evening and morning at the Vatican on November 1, 1954, when the ancient picture of Mary (sometimes wrongly attributed to St. Luke) in the Basilica of St. Mary Major was crowned with a golden crown and Mary's Feast of her Queenship was established by Pope Pius XII. I was invited by Cardinal Pizzardo, one of the senior cardinals in charge of universities and seminaries throughout the world, to be his secretary. So that meant being with him in his apartment at which he personally fed the crowd gathered there and the next morning going as his attendant in procession into St. Peter's Basilica during the Mass and afterward viewing the large crowd from the balcony in front of St. Peter's. It was an unforgettable moment.

We have, of course, no direct quotations from Scripture to support this feast. Nothing, that is, unless we accept the statements in the Annunciation that Mary would be the Mother of God, and from that flows the fact that she is esteemed as Queen of Angels and of Men and Women. As mentioned before, everything flows from Mary's dignity in her Annunciation and the following Mysteries as Mother of God.

What is required is that we look on Mary as totally the work of God. It was in view of universal salvation that she was preserved from original sin from the first moment of her conception. And it was because she was the Mother of God that she was regarded as Queen of Angels and of Men and Women. That follows naturally on her mothership of God, and anything less would not be the honor due her.

What application does this feast have for our personal lives? Well, let us return to the apparitions of Mary, for example to that of the Miraculous Medal at the Chapel of Rue de Bac in Paris in 1830. I have called this a preparation for the dogma which was declared in 1854, the dogma of the Immaculate Conception. Why do I say that? Simply because, in the apparition and again in the metal, we see clearly these words, "O Mary conceived without sin, pray for us who have recourse to thee."

Then again, at Lourdes, Mary declared herself to be "the Immaculate Conception," an expression which Bernadette did not at all understand because she had never heard of the dogma five years previously.

To these two appearances of Mary can be added that of Our Lady of Guadalupe in 1531 at Mexico City, in which she left an image of herself in a maternity outfit on the *tilma* of Juan Diego. Finally, there are the appearances of Mary at Medjugorje ever since the first apparition in 1981, and especially the fact that Mary had declared that these are her final apparitions on earth. Does that mean that the world is coming to its end and Jesus will be glorified? I don't know, but certain signs of the times point to it, for if this is not the century in which Satan is loosed for a time (Rev 20:7-10), then I don't know what we must wait for. No, let us remain under the protection of Mary as Queen of Angels and of Men and Women.

# Conclusion

I have completed this study of the mysteries, including the additional Fruitful Mysteries, and it is time to make a few concluding remarks.

I have had two thoughts in mind throughout this study: (1) That those who say the Rosary should meditate on the mysteries instead of paying attention to the Hail Marys being recited. After all, the Hail Marys simply give the amount of time during which we contemplate the Mysteries involved. (2) It seems to me that we go directly from the Infancy Gospel to the Passion Account, simply omitting altogether the three years of Jesus' public ministry. Why is this? Well, in my own opinion, it reflects the condition of Catholics when the Rosary was first used. At that time, people generally could not read or write, hence the Hail Marys were limited to one hundred and fifty to correspond with the number of psalms in the Divine Office or breviary, with which the Rosary was compared. That is just a guess, of course, and may be entirely wrong. But what is important now that Catholics are educated and well-read is to recognize that Jesus spent three very important years of public life among us and include them in our Rosary.

If it be asked how we would fit this new ordering of the Rosary to our saying of it every week, let me repeat my suggestion that we begin on Sunday with the Joyful Mysteries, continue with the Fruitful on Monday, the Sorrowful on

Tuesday, and the Glorious on Wednesday. Thus at least once a week, we would be saying all four parts of the Rosary.

Now, let me give a bit of personal witness. Since I have been saying the Fruitful Mysteries over the past several years, I have been greatly helped. I think that all one needs to do is pause a moment to think about what mysteries are included in the Fruitful Ones and the reason will be apparent. At any rate, there is no intention to go counter to the teachings of the Church in any way. Our purpose is to include the Fruitful Mysteries as a help, not as a source of vexation, and to include the two additional ages of meditation on the other mysteries. May it be helpful in our veneration of our Blessed Mother, instead of the opposite.